Book Title:

"From Dreams to Reality: A Cafe Diary"

"Sustainable Success: Building a Dream Cafe in Vancouver"

By Jenny Koo

Imprint: Independently published.

Copyright © 2024 by Jenny K. Koo. All rights reserved.

No part of this book may be used or reproduced in any manner whatsoever without written permission.

For information, please email to jennykookk@gmail.com

"From Dreams to Reality: A Cafe Diary - Sustainable Success: Building a Dream Cafe in Vancouver"

By Jenny Koo

Table of Contents

Title: *From Dreams to Reality: A Cafe Diary*
Subtitle: *Sustainable Success: Building a Dream Cafe in Vancouver*

1. **The Dream Begins**
   - Introduction to Koo San and her vision.
   - Early inspirations and the first steps toward opening a cafe.
   - Challenges and uncertainties faced at the beginning of the journey.
2. **Research and Planning**
   - The impact of COVID-19 on the cafe industry.
   - Strategic research on sustainability and business planning.

- Overcoming doubts and finding ways to adapt to a post-pandemic world.

3. **Finding the Perfect Location**
    - The challenges of finding a suitable location in Vancouver.
    - Weighing pros and cons of potential sites.
    - Securing a location and preparing for renovations.

4. **Designing the Cafe**
    - Collaborating with designers and architects.
    - Creating a sustainable, inviting space.
    - Decisions on seating plans, layout, and operational efficiency.

5. **Navigating Permits and Regulations**
    - The bureaucratic hurdles of obtaining permits and licenses.
    - Managing inspections and ensuring compliance with city regulations.
    - Addressing unexpected issues and staying on track.

6. **Building a Team**
    - Recruiting staff who share the vision and values of the cafe.
    - Training and optimizing the team for maximum efficiency.
    - Determining operational hours, staffing needs, and pricing strategies.

7. **Sourcing Sustainable Ingredients**
    - Building relationships with local suppliers and farmers.

- Balancing quality and cost with sustainable practices.
- Creating a menu that reflects the cafe's commitment to sustainability.

8. **Marketing and Promotion**

   - Developing a strong brand identity.
   - Engaging with the local community and building anticipation.
   - Strategies for attracting customers and ensuring repeat business.

9. **Overcoming Setbacks**

   - Dealing with unexpected challenges during the final stages.
   - Staying motivated and adapting to last-minute changes.
   - Lessons learned and the importance of flexibility.

10. **Grand Opening**

    - The final preparations and the emotions leading up to the grand opening.
    - The opening day experience and customer feedback.
    - Reflections on the journey and plans for the future.

Bonus: Coffee Tasting Journal Template

Chapter 1: The Dream Begins

Diary Entry: January 3rd, 2021

It's a chilly Vancouver morning, the kind that makes you crave a hot cup of something comforting. I've just finished my shift at one of the many jobs I juggle—today was at the bookstore, tomorrow it'll be the late-night diner down the street. I'm not complaining; these jobs have kept me afloat, and each one has given me something to learn. But lately, something inside me has been stirring, a restlessness that no amount of work seems to satisfy.

I think back to my school days, how I used to be so full of energy, always the one who could chat up a storm with anyone who crossed my path. Back then, I was that girl who loved meeting new people, who thrived in the hustle and bustle of life. I traveled whenever I could, soaking in the sights, sounds, and, most importantly, the flavors of the world. Each country I visited left a mark on me, and each culture taught me something new.

But time has changed me. It's not that I don't enjoy people's company anymore—it's just that the energy it takes to engage in small talk now feels like a luxury I can't afford. Maybe it's all these years of working multiple jobs, or maybe it's just life molding me into someone different. These days, I'm more about actions than words, more focused on working hard and achieving something tangible. Less talk, more work—that's my mantra now. I think they call it being an ambivert, but honestly, I just feel like someone who's seen enough to know that life isn't always about being the loudest in the room.

Growing up here in Vancouver, I've learned to appreciate its quiet beauty. This city has been my constant, my home base, even as my dreams have carried me across the globe in search of something more. And now, it's where I want to build something of my own. A cafe—my cafe.

I've always loved cafes. They're places where people connect, where cultures blend over a cup of coffee or tea. The idea of creating a space where people can feel at home, where they can enjoy a moment of peace in their busy lives, has always appealed to me. But it's more than that. I want to build something sustainable, something that gives back to this city that has given me so much. A cafe that respects the environment, supports local farmers, and serves as a hub for the community.

But where do I even start?

I've saved up a bit from working all these jobs—enough to start thinking seriously about this dream. But every time I try to take a step forward, I'm hit with a wall of uncertainty. I have no idea how much it will actually cost to open and run a cafe, or what kind of licenses and permits I'll need. The more I think about it, the more daunting it seems. And yet, the dream doesn't fade. It's there, persistent, in the back of my mind, urging me to take the leap.

Maybe today's the day I start. I don't know exactly how, but I think the first step is admitting to myself that this dream isn't going to go away. I need to face it, plan it, and, most importantly, believe that I can do it.

Diary Entry: January 10th, 2021

It's been a week since I made the decision to go after this dream, and I've done little more than scribble down ideas in this notebook. I can't lie, I'm scared. Scared of failing, scared of losing everything I've worked so hard for. But I keep telling myself that every big journey starts with a single step, right?

So, I started researching. I didn't know where to begin, so I just googled "how to start a cafe" and ended up with about a million results. Some of it is overwhelming, but some of it is exactly what I needed to read. I've found a few online communities and forums where people share their experiences, and that's been helpful. Reading about others who've been where I am now makes me feel less alone.

Today, I made a list. It's a rough draft of all the things I think I need to figure out before I can open the doors to my cafe. I wrote down everything from finding a location to figuring out the menu, sourcing ingredients, and even the kind of vibe I want the cafe to have. There's so much to do, but seeing it all on paper somehow makes it feel more manageable.

The biggest challenge right now is money. I've been saving for years, but it's still not enough. I've been thinking about whether I should take out a loan or find investors, but both options terrify me. I've never been in debt, and the thought of owing money makes my stomach churn. But at the same time, I know that if I want this dream to become a reality, I'll have to take some risks.

I don't know what's going to happen next, but I'm committed. This cafe isn't just a passing fancy; it's what I've been working toward for years, even if I didn't realize it until now. It's the culmination of all my experiences, all the jobs I've worked, all the people I've met. I'm doing this. One step at a time.

Diary Entry: January 18th, 2021
I took a walk around the city today, letting the familiar streets of Vancouver clear my mind. I visited a few of my favorite cafes, not just for the coffee, but to observe. I watched the way the baristas interacted with customers, how the spaces were laid out, and the kind of people who frequented each place. It struck me how each cafe had its own personality, its own vibe that either drew you in or made you feel like you didn't quite belong.

That's what I want to create—a place that feels like home to everyone who steps inside. A cafe where people can come to escape the rain, enjoy a warm drink, and maybe even strike up a conversation with a stranger. But how do I make that happen? How do I make people feel welcome in a way that's genuine and not just good marketing?

As I sat in one of these cafes, sipping on my latte, I realized that I'm not just building a business—I'm creating a community. This cafe is more than just a place to sell coffee; it's a space where people will connect, relax, and maybe even find a little piece of themselves. That's what I want to offer: a space where people can slow down, if only for a few minutes.

But before I can even think about the design or the vibe, there's the practical side of things. Today, I started making calls. I contacted a few local businesses and asked if they'd be willing to chat about their experiences. Some were surprisingly open, offering advice on everything from managing employees to navigating Vancouver's strict business regulations. Others were less helpful, probably seeing me as just another dreamer who wouldn't last in this tough industry.

Still, every conversation taught me something. For one, I learned that Vancouver's real estate market is as brutal as I'd feared. Finding a location that fits my vision and budget is going to be one of my biggest challenges. But I'm determined to find the right spot—a place that's not just affordable but also has the potential to draw in the kind of community I want to build.

Diary Entry: January 24th, 2021

I spent the last few days diving into the numbers. Budgets, costs, financial projections—it's all so much more complicated than I'd imagined. I started with the basics, like estimating the cost of rent, utilities, and equipment. But the more I dig, the more I realize how much I don't know. It feels like I'm piecing together a puzzle without knowing what the final picture is supposed to look like.

One thing I've learned is that I'll need to be extremely careful with my spending. My savings, while substantial for someone who's worked multiple jobs for years, will only go so far. I've been looking into government grants and programs that support small businesses, especially those focused on sustainability. There are a few promising options, but they all come with strings attached—deadlines, application processes, and, of course, competition from other hopeful entrepreneurs.

Then there's the issue of cash flow. I've read countless stories about cafes that had a great start but failed because they couldn't maintain steady income. It's a terrifying thought—that even if I manage to open the doors, keeping them open is an entirely different battle. I need to plan for the lean times, the months when business might be slow, and make sure I have a financial cushion to fall back on.

The idea of taking out a loan keeps looming in the back of my mind. It's a step I'm hesitant to take, but it might be necessary if I want to do this right. I'm still undecided, though. I want to exhaust all other options before committing to something that could put me in debt for years. Maybe I'll reach out to a financial advisor—someone who can help me navigate these waters with a clearer head.

Diary Entry: January 31st, 2021

I had a conversation with an old friend today, someone I haven't seen in years. We met up at a small cafe that's been around for ages, one of those places that feels like it's part of the city's fabric. Over coffee, I told her about my plans. She was surprised, but supportive—she always knew I had a passion for something more than just the routine jobs I've been doing.

She asked me a question that's been stuck in my mind all day: *"What will your cafe stand for?"* It's a simple question, but one that made me pause. I've been so focused on the logistics, the how-to's of starting a business, that I hadn't fully articulated the why. Yes, I want to create a space that brings people together, but what is the deeper meaning behind it? What values will my cafe represent?

Sustainability, of course. That's been a guiding principle from the start. I want my cafe to minimize its environmental impact, to source locally and ethically, and to inspire others to think about their own choices. But there's more to it than that. I want my cafe to be a place of inclusivity, where everyone feels welcome, no matter who they are or where they come from. A space that reflects the diversity of Vancouver itself, with a menu that celebrates global flavors and local ingredients.

This conversation has sparked something in me—a clearer vision of what I want this cafe to be. It's more than just a dream now; it's a mission. I don't just want to succeed in business—I want to create something meaningful, something that adds value to the community and leaves a positive mark on the city I love.

So, what will my cafe stand for? It will stand for sustainability, inclusivity, and community. It will be a place where everyone is welcome, where the coffee is as ethical as it is delicious, and where people can come together to share, learn, and connect.

I still have so much to figure out, but this feels like a breakthrough. I have a vision, and now I just need to make it real.

Chapter 1 Summary and Next Steps:
Koo San has begun her journey by acknowledging her dream and starting to take concrete steps toward making it a reality. She's faced with the challenge of balancing her vision with the practicalities of starting a business, but she's committed to creating a cafe that stands for more than just good coffee—it's about building a sustainable, inclusive community space.

In the next chapter, "Research and Planning," we'll delve into the details of how she begins to gather the knowledge and resources she needs. She'll start to learn about the cafe industry, explore sustainable practices, and begin crafting a business plan.

Chapter 2: Research and Planning

Diary Entry: February 7th, 2021

I woke up this morning with a sinking feeling in my stomach. I've been trying to stay positive, but the news these days makes it hard. Every time I turn on the TV or check my phone, I'm bombarded with stories about businesses struggling to stay afloat, not just here in Vancouver, but around the world. It's hard to ignore the reality that we're living through unprecedented times—times when even the most established businesses are closing their doors for good.

The global pandemic has wreaked havoc on so many lives and industries. Shops, cafes, and restaurants that once buzzed with life are now empty or shut down altogether. Borders are closed, travel is restricted, and people are working from home, avoiding public spaces as much as possible. The social gatherings that were once the heartbeat of cafes have been voided by social distancing measures. It's not the world I imagined when I first dreamt of opening my cafe.

I can't help but ask myself: Should I still go through with this? Is it even possible to start a new business in the middle of a global crisis that's already claimed so many?

The fear of failure looms larger than ever. The statistics are terrifying—so many small businesses have gone bankrupt, unable to withstand the economic blows dealt by COVID-19. Starting a cafe, in particular, seems risky when people are spending more time at home, and the idea of sitting in a cozy cafe with strangers feels almost irresponsible in the current climate.

But then again, this pandemic won't last forever, will it? Eventually, life will return to some semblance of normalcy. People will crave connection again, the warmth of a community space, and the comfort of a favorite spot to sip coffee and unwind. I have to believe that.

So, what can I do? How can I move forward with this dream in a way that makes sense given the world we're living in?

Diary Entry: February 12th, 2021

I spent the last few days digging deep into research, trying to understand how businesses are adapting to the pandemic and what I can learn from their experiences. The more I read, the clearer it becomes that adaptability is key. Businesses that have survived—some even thrived—during these tough times are the ones that were quick to pivot, to think outside the box, and to meet their customers where they are now, not where they were before the world turned upside down.

One of the most important things I've learned is that flexibility is crucial. I need to build a business model that can withstand uncertainty and change. This means considering new ways of operating that don't solely rely on in-person interactions. For example, I've been looking into the possibility of incorporating a strong online presence for my cafe. Offering online orders, delivery services, and even creating virtual events or workshops could help maintain a connection with customers, even if they can't physically be in the cafe.

I've also been researching the concept of a "pandemic-proof" business. It's about creating a space that is not just safe but also appealing in the current climate. This might mean investing in outdoor seating, ensuring excellent ventilation, or even rethinking the layout to allow for more social distancing. I'm considering a hybrid model that balances a cozy, inviting atmosphere with the practical needs of a post-pandemic world.

Another aspect I'm exploring is how to integrate sustainable practices that are also cost-effective in these uncertain times. The pandemic has made many people more conscious of their choices, and I believe that a cafe focused on sustainability—using local, organic ingredients, minimizing waste, and supporting the community—could resonate even more now than before. People want to support businesses that align with their values, especially when those businesses are contributing to the recovery and resilience of the local economy.

Diary Entry: February 19th, 2021

Today was a turning point. After a lot of reflection and research, I've realized that the pandemic, while undoubtedly a challenge, doesn't have to be the end of my dream. If anything, it's made me more determined to create something that can survive and thrive in a world that's changed so drastically.

I've decided that my cafe will be built with resilience in mind. I'll focus on creating a flexible business model that can adapt to whatever the future holds. I'll prioritize health and safety without sacrificing the warmth and community feel that I want my cafe to have. And most importantly, I'll stay true to the core values of sustainability and inclusivity that have driven this dream from the start.

There's no denying that the road ahead is uncertain, and the risks are high. But I'm choosing to see this as an opportunity to build something stronger, something that can weather the storms and come out the other side better for it.

My next steps are clear: I need to continue researching, but now with a focus on businesses that have successfully navigated the pandemic. I'll start drafting a business plan that includes contingency strategies for future disruptions. And I'll begin networking with other entrepreneurs who have walked this path before me, learning from their successes and mistakes.

This dream isn't just about opening a cafe anymore—it's about building something meaningful and lasting, no matter what the world throws at it. I'm ready for the challenge.

Chapter 2 Summary and Next Steps:

In Chapter 2, Koo San faces the harsh realities of the COVID-19 pandemic and the impact it has had on the global economy and local businesses. The pandemic forces her to question the viability of her dream, but through careful research and reflection, she decides to proceed with a flexible, resilient approach. She begins to plan for a cafe that can adapt to the uncertainties of the future, while still staying true to her core values.

The next chapter, "Finding the Perfect Location," will explore how she navigates the challenging real estate market in Vancouver, with these new considerations in mind. She'll be looking for a space that not only fits her vision but also meets the demands of a post-pandemic world.

Chapter 3: Finding the Perfect Location

Diary Entry: February 26th, 2021

The search for the perfect location has officially begun. I spent most of today walking through different neighborhoods in Vancouver, trying to imagine where my cafe could thrive. It's both exciting and nerve-wracking—every time I see a "For Lease" sign, my heart skips a beat. Could this be the place where my dream comes to life?

Vancouver's real estate market is notoriously difficult, and the pandemic has only added to the uncertainty. Some areas that used to be bustling with life are now eerily quiet, with many storefronts empty or boarded up. It's disheartening to see how many businesses have had to close their doors, and it serves as a stark reminder of the risks involved in starting a new venture. But I can't let fear hold me back. I know that if I find the right spot, it could make all the difference.

Today, I focused on a few key neighborhoods: Mount Pleasant, Kitsilano, and Commercial Drive. Each of these areas has its own unique vibe and community, and I want to choose a location that feels like the right fit not just for the business, but for the people who live there.

Diary Entry: March 3rd, 2021

I visited a few potential locations over the past week, and while none of them felt quite right, the process has taught me a lot about what I'm looking for. The first place I saw was in Kitsilano—a small, charming storefront on a quiet street. It had big windows that let in plenty of natural light, and I could immediately picture the cafe bustling with customers. But as I looked closer, I noticed some issues. The space was small, maybe too small, and the layout was awkward, with a narrow entrance that might make social distancing difficult.

Next, I toured a spot in Mount Pleasant. This one was larger, with a more open layout that I could easily see transforming into a welcoming cafe. The area is trendy, with a lot of foot traffic and a diverse community that I think would appreciate a sustainable, inclusive cafe. But the rent was sky-high, and with the pandemic still casting a shadow over everything, I couldn't justify the cost. It would have left me with little room in the budget for anything else, and I'm not willing to take that risk.

The last location I saw was on Commercial Drive. This neighborhood is known for its eclectic mix of cultures and vibrant street life. The space itself was in an older building, full of character but in need of some serious renovation. The landlord seemed eager to make a deal, probably because they've struggled to find tenants during the pandemic. Part of me is tempted by the potential of this place—the high ceilings, the exposed brick walls—but the amount of work it would require is daunting. I'd need to invest a significant amount of money just to get it up to code, let alone turn it into the cafe of my dreams.

I left each location with a mix of hope and doubt. It's becoming clear that finding the perfect spot is going to be harder than I thought. But I'm not giving up. I've already learned so much from these visits, and I'm beginning to refine what I want and need from this space.

Diary Entry: March 10th, 2021

After days of searching and countless phone calls, I found a location that might just be the one. It's in Mount Pleasant, on a corner lot with great visibility. The building is modern, with large windows that overlook the street, allowing plenty of light to stream in—perfect for creating the warm, inviting atmosphere I want for the cafe. The layout is open and flexible, with enough space for a comfortable seating area, a well-designed counter, and even some outdoor seating, which is crucial given the current pandemic.

The rent is still a concern. It's not cheap, but it's more reasonable than some of the other places I've seen, and the landlord seems willing to negotiate. I'm also considering the long-term potential. Mount Pleasant is an area that's continuing to grow and attract new businesses, which could mean more foot traffic and a stable customer base.

But it's not just about the numbers—it's about the feel of the place. When I stood inside the empty space today, I could imagine it filled with the smell of freshly brewed coffee, the sound of conversations and laughter, and the sight of people finding a moment of peace in their day. That vision, more than anything else, is what's pushing me to seriously consider this spot.

I've made an appointment to meet with the landlord and discuss terms. I'm nervous, but I know that this is a crucial step in making my dream a reality. If we can reach an agreement that makes financial sense, this could be the beginning of something incredible.

Diary Entry: March 15th, 2021

The meeting with the landlord went better than I expected. We talked about my vision for the cafe, and he seemed genuinely interested and supportive. I could tell he's had trouble finding tenants during the pandemic, which put me in a stronger position to negotiate. In the end, we reached a deal that feels fair. The rent is within my budget, and I managed to get a few months of reduced rent to help me get started. It's a small victory, but it feels huge.

I spent the afternoon walking around Mount Pleasant, imagining what it will be like to finally open the doors to my cafe. The area is full of young professionals, families, and creatives—exactly the kind of community I want to serve. There's a mix of old and new, with modern condos next to historic homes, and independent shops lining the streets. I can see my cafe fitting right in, offering a space where people can come together, even in these challenging times.

Of course, there are still so many things to figure out—permits, renovations, and a thousand other details. But for the first time in weeks, I feel a sense of clarity. I have a location, a place to call my own. Now, the real work begins.

Diary Entry: March 22nd, 2021

I signed the lease today. It feels surreal, like I'm walking on air and yet weighed down by the enormity of what I've just committed to. This space is mine now, for better or worse, and it's up to me to turn it into the cafe I've been dreaming about for so long.

There's a lot of work ahead—more than I probably realize—but I'm ready to tackle it one step at a time. The first order of business is to start planning the renovations. The space is in good shape, but I want to make it special. I've already started sketching out ideas for the layout, thinking about how to create a flow that feels natural and inviting, and where to place the counter, seating, and decor.

I'm also thinking about the pandemic and how to make the space safe for everyone. I'll need to incorporate plenty of ventilation, consider touchless payment options, and ensure that the layout allows for social distancing without losing the cozy, welcoming atmosphere I want. It's a balancing act, but I'm determined to get it right.

There's a lot to do, but for now, I'm just going to take a moment to breathe it all in. I have a location. I have a space where my dream can take root and grow. It's scary, but it's also exhilarating. This is the beginning of something new, something that feels like it was meant to be.

Chapter 3 Summary and Next Steps:

Koo San has found a location for her cafe in the vibrant neighborhood of Mount Pleasant. The process of searching for the perfect spot was filled with challenges and tough decisions, but she has secured a space that meets her needs and fits her vision. Now that she has the location, the next step is to move forward with designing the cafe, ensuring that it reflects her values of sustainability, inclusivity, and safety in a post-pandemic world.

In the next chapter, "Designing the Cafe," Koo San will collaborate with designers and architects to transform the space into the cafe of her dreams. She'll face the challenge of balancing aesthetics with functionality, choosing eco-friendly materials, and making decisions that will shape the atmosphere and identity of the cafe.

Chapter 4: Designing the Cafe

Diary Entry: March 29th, 2021

Now that I have the location, it's time to turn this empty space into a cafe that not only looks beautiful but also embodies everything I stand for. I've spent the last few days researching design firms and architects, trying to find someone who understands my vision for sustainability and inclusivity. It's not just about making the place look good; it's about creating a space that feels good, too—a place that's warm, welcoming, and in harmony with the environment.

After a few interviews, I finally found a design team that I think will be the perfect fit. They specialize in sustainable design and have experience working with small businesses, particularly cafes and restaurants. What drew me to them was their passion for using eco-friendly materials and their ability to blend functionality with aesthetics. They seem to really get what I'm trying to achieve—creating a space that's not only visually appealing but also practical and environmentally responsible.

We've scheduled our first official meeting to go over ideas and start sketching out the initial design. I'm excited but also nervous. This is the part where everything starts to become real—where my ideas are put to the test, and I have to make decisions that will define the look and feel of my cafe.

Diary Entry: April 5th, 2021

I met with the design team today, and we spent hours going over every detail of the cafe. We talked about everything from the layout to the color scheme, to the type of furniture and fixtures we'll use. The goal is to create a space that feels both modern and timeless, with a cozy, inviting atmosphere that makes people want to linger.

One of the first things we discussed was the layout. The space is essentially a blank canvas, which gives us a lot of flexibility, but it also means we have to be very intentional about how we use every square foot. The team suggested dividing the space into distinct areas— one for the counter and coffee preparation, one for seating, and one for a small retail section where we can sell locally sourced products, like coffee beans, teas, and eco-friendly merchandise.

I'm especially excited about the seating area. We're planning to include a mix of comfortable chairs, communal tables, and window seats, so there's a spot for everyone, whether they're meeting friends, working on their laptop, or just enjoying a quiet moment with a book. We're also incorporating some flexible seating options, like movable benches and stools, to make the space adaptable for different events or gatherings.

We talked a lot about materials, too. I'm committed to using sustainable, eco-friendly options wherever possible. We're looking at reclaimed wood for the tables and counters, bamboo flooring, and low-VOC paints to ensure good indoor air quality. Even the light fixtures will be energy-efficient, with LED bulbs and natural lighting where possible.

The team also suggested some creative ideas for decor—like using living plants to bring a touch of nature indoors, and incorporating local art to add character and support the community. I love the idea of having a "living wall" of plants behind the counter, which would not only look stunning but also improve air quality and create a calming atmosphere.

We're also thinking about how to design the space in a way that's mindful of the ongoing pandemic. This means ensuring plenty of ventilation, providing enough space between tables for social distancing, and considering touchless options for things like doors and faucets. We're even exploring the idea of having an outdoor seating area, which would be a safer option for customers who might still be wary of indoor spaces.

Today's meeting left me feeling both excited and overwhelmed. There are so many decisions to make, and I want to get everything just right. But I also know that this process is about more than just creating a beautiful space—it's about creating a place that reflects my values and serves the community.

Diary Entry: April 12th, 2021

The design process is moving forward, and today we started finalizing some of the key elements of the cafe's interior. The team presented a few different color palettes, and after much deliberation, we decided on a combination of earthy tones—soft greens, warm browns, and gentle creams. These colors will create a calm, welcoming environment that feels connected to nature, which is exactly the vibe I want to convey.

We also selected the furniture today. I've opted for a mix of styles—some modern, sleek pieces to keep the space looking fresh, and some more rustic, reclaimed items that add warmth and character. The tables will be made from reclaimed wood, each one unique, with its own story to tell. The chairs will be a mix of comfortable armchairs and simpler wooden stools, with plenty of cushions and throws to make the space feel cozy.

One of the biggest challenges we discussed was how to make the cafe both sustainable and cost-effective. Some of the eco-friendly materials are more expensive, and I'm already working within a tight budget. But I'm determined not to compromise on sustainability. The design team has been great about finding creative solutions—like sourcing local materials and working with suppliers who offer discounts for small businesses committed to green practices.

We've also been talking about the cafe's branding and how the design can reflect its identity. I want the space to feel like an extension of the brand—sustainable, inclusive, and community-oriented. We're playing with ideas for signage and artwork that will highlight these values, like a mural that tells the story of the cafe's journey, or signs that educate customers about the sustainability practices we're implementing.

The outdoor seating area is something I'm particularly excited about. We've decided to create a small patio space with tables and chairs, surrounded by planters filled with native plants. It'll be a lovely spot for customers to enjoy their coffee in the fresh air, and it gives us an extra layer of safety during the pandemic. I can already picture it—a little oasis in the middle of the city, where people can relax and recharge.

Diary Entry: April 18th, 2021

Today was a big day—we finalized the design! After weeks of planning, sketching, and reworking ideas, we have a complete blueprint for the cafe. It's everything I envisioned and more. The space will be warm, welcoming, and full of character, with every detail carefully thought out to create a positive experience for everyone who walks through the door.

We're starting construction next week, and while I know it's going to be a lot of work, I'm eager to see the space come to life. There will undoubtedly be challenges along the way—delays, unexpected costs, and all the usual hiccups that come with renovations—but I'm ready for them. This is the part where the dream starts to become reality.

As I prepare for the next steps, I'm reminded of why I'm doing this. It's not just about opening a cafe; it's about creating a place that brings people together, supports the community, and makes a positive impact on the environment. I'm building something that I hope will outlast the pandemic, something that will be a part of this city for years to come.

Diary Entry: April 25th, 2021

The construction crew arrived today, and the transformation has begun. The space is a flurry of activity—walls being painted, floors being installed, and furniture being assembled. It's amazing to see the designs we've been working on for weeks finally start to take shape. The bare bones of the cafe are gradually filling in, and with each passing day, it feels more and more like the place I've imagined.

I've been spending as much time as I can on-site, overseeing the work and making sure everything is going according to plan. It's exhausting, but also incredibly rewarding. There's something magical about seeing your vision come to life, piece by piece.

Of course, there have been a few hiccups already—delays in getting certain materials, a miscommunication about the layout of the counter—but nothing we haven't been able to resolve. The design team and the construction crew have been fantastic, working closely with me to make adjustments and keep everything on track.

One of the things I'm most excited about is the living wall behind the counter. The crew started installing it today, and even though it's not finished yet, it's already stunning. The wall will be filled with a variety of plants, carefully chosen to thrive indoors and improve air quality. It's going to be the focal point of the cafe, a reminder of the natural world and the importance of sustainability. I can't wait to see it in full bloom.

We're still on track to finish the renovations in a few weeks, which means I need to start thinking about the next steps—hiring staff, sourcing ingredients, and finalizing the menu. There's so much to do, but I'm ready. Every day brings me closer to opening the doors and welcoming the first customers into this space I've worked so hard to create.

Chapter 4 Summary and Next Steps:

In Chapter 4, Koo San collaborates with a design team to transform her chosen location into a sustainable, welcoming cafe. She makes important decisions about the layout, materials, and aesthetics, all while keeping her commitment to sustainability at the forefront. The chapter ends with the start of construction, marking a significant milestone in her journey.

The next chapter, "Navigating Permits and Regulations," will explore the bureaucratic challenges Koo San faces as she works to get everything approved and ready for the grand opening. She'll encounter inspections, licensing issues, and the frustrations that come with dealing with city regulations, but she'll also experience the relief of seeing it all come together.

Chapter 5: Navigating Permits and Regulations

Diary Entry: May 2nd, 2021

The construction is well underway, and with the space starting to take shape, I'm turning my attention to the less glamorous—but absolutely crucial—side of opening a business: permits and regulations. I knew from the start that this was going to be one of the biggest hurdles, but now that I'm in the thick of it, I'm realizing just how overwhelming it can be.

Vancouver is known for its strict business regulations, especially when it comes to food and beverage establishments. There are health permits, building permits, business licenses, fire safety approvals, and so many other things to consider. Each one comes with its own set of requirements, forms, and fees. It's a lot to manage, and the thought of missing something critical keeps me up at night.

I've been spending hours poring over the city's website, trying to make sure I understand every requirement. It's like navigating a maze—one wrong turn, and you're back at the beginning. I've started compiling a checklist to keep everything organized: health inspection, fire safety clearance, zoning compliance, building codes, and the list goes on. Each step is interconnected; without one, I can't move forward with the next.

Today, I submitted the initial application for my business license. It's just the first of many steps, but it feels good to have started. I know the process can take weeks, sometimes even months, depending on how smoothly things go. I'm bracing myself for potential delays, but I'm also determined to stay on top of everything.

Diary Entry: May 9th, 2021

The first hurdle came sooner than I expected. I received a call from the city's health department today—they need to conduct a preliminary inspection before I can move forward with the next stage of the process. I've been told that health inspections can be notoriously difficult to pass, especially on the first try. The inspector will be looking at everything from the kitchen layout to the type of equipment I'm using, and even the materials we're incorporating into the design. If anything is out of place, it could mean costly changes and delays.

I spent the rest of the day in a bit of a panic, reviewing the plans with the design team and making sure everything is up to code. The construction crew has been great about working with us to ensure that we're meeting all the necessary standards, but there's still a lot of uncertainty. Even a small oversight could set us back, and with the grand opening inching closer, the pressure is on.

One of the biggest concerns is the ventilation system. Given the pandemic, air quality and circulation have become even more critical. We've designed the cafe with this in mind, but the inspector will be scrutinizing every detail to ensure that the system is not only efficient but also compliant with the latest health guidelines.

I've scheduled the inspection for next week, and all I can do now is prepare as thoroughly as possible and hope for the best. It's stressful, but I know that this is a necessary part of the process. Once we pass this hurdle, we'll be one step closer to making the cafe a reality.

Diary Entry: May 16th, 2021

The health inspection happened today, and I'm relieved to say that it went better than expected. The inspector was thorough, going through every inch of the kitchen and seating area, but in the end, we passed with only a few minor issues to address. There are some adjustments needed to the sink placement and additional signage required for health and safety, but overall, it's nothing we can't handle. The inspector even complimented our attention to detail, especially when it came to the ventilation system—a huge relief!

With the health inspection out of the way, I can move forward with the next steps: obtaining the fire safety clearance and finalizing the building permits. Each of these steps is essential, and each one brings its own set of challenges. I've already contacted the fire department to schedule an inspection, and I've started gathering the necessary documents for the building permits.

The fire inspection is another big one. Vancouver's fire codes are strict, especially for businesses like cafes where cooking and heating equipment are used. The fire marshal will be looking at our exits, fire suppression systems, and emergency plans. It's nerve-wracking, but I'm trying to stay positive. The design team has been fantastic, ensuring that everything meets the required standards, so I'm hopeful that this will go smoothly.

There's also the issue of zoning. My cafe is located in a commercial zone, which is good, but there are specific regulations about the type of business that can operate in certain areas. I've been assured that we're in compliance, but I need to get official confirmation before moving forward. The last thing I want is to get caught up in a zoning dispute that could delay the opening by months.

Diary Entry: May 23rd, 2021

I'm starting to feel like I'm in a constant battle with bureaucracy. Today, I ran into an issue with the building permits. It turns out that the original plans we submitted didn't account for a few minor changes we made during the design process—like the addition of the living wall and some alterations to the kitchen layout. Because of this, we need to submit revised plans and wait for approval before we can continue with certain aspects of the construction.

It's frustrating, to say the least. I feel like I'm constantly jumping through hoops, trying to meet every regulation and requirement, only to find out that there's another hurdle just around the corner. But I also know that this is part of the process—part of making sure that everything is done right.

I spent the afternoon working with the design team to update the plans and resubmit them to the city. We're doing everything we can to expedite the process, but I'm mentally preparing for a delay. I keep reminding myself that it's better to get everything sorted out now than to rush and face bigger problems down the line.

The fire inspection is scheduled for later this week, and I'm hoping that at least that will go smoothly. If we can get through that without any major issues, it will be a huge weight off my shoulders.

Diary Entry: May 30th, 2021

The fire inspection is complete, and I'm thrilled to say that we passed! The fire marshal was thorough, but everything was up to code. The fire exits are clearly marked, the suppression system is in place, and our emergency plan was approved. This is a big win, and it means we're one step closer to opening the doors.

However, we're still waiting on the revised building permits. The delay is frustrating, especially since we're so close to the finish line. I've been in constant contact with the city, pushing for updates, but these things take time. It's a lesson in patience—a reminder that even when you do everything right, there are still factors beyond your control.

To keep myself from going crazy with the waiting, I've been focusing on the details that I can control—like finalizing the menu, sourcing the last few pieces of furniture, and starting to think about the staff I'll need to hire. It's a way to stay productive and keep the momentum going, even when the red tape threatens to slow everything down.

One bright spot in all of this has been the support I've received from the community. Word has started to spread about the cafe, and I've had people stop by the site, asking about the opening date and expressing their excitement. It's a reminder of why I'm doing this—why all the stress and frustration is worth it. I'm not just opening a business; I'm creating a space for people, for the community, for connection.

I'm still holding on to the hope that we'll get the permits approved soon and that we'll be able to stay on schedule. But whatever happens, I know that we'll make it work. This dream is too important to give up on.

Chapter 5 Summary and Next Steps:

In Chapter 5, Koo San navigates the complex and often frustrating process of securing permits and approvals necessary to open her cafe. She faces challenges with health inspections, fire safety regulations, and building permits, but her perseverance and attention to detail help her overcome these hurdles. The chapter ends with the fire inspection passed, but the wait for building permits continues, highlighting the importance of patience and determination in the journey to opening her cafe.

The next chapter, "Building a Team," will focus on the process of hiring staff who share Koo San's vision and values. She'll face the challenge of finding the right people to help bring her dream to life, and she'll work on creating a positive and supportive work environment that reflects the inclusive, community-oriented spirit of the cafe.

Chapter 6: Building a Team

Diary Entry: June 1st, 2021

With the construction nearing completion, it's time to focus on assembling the team that will help me bring this cafe to life. I've spent so much time on the design and logistics that the reality of hiring staff has only just started to sink in. This is the team that will be the face of my cafe, the ones who will interact with customers every day, and it's crucial that they share my vision and values.

I've been thinking a lot about how to optimize the business for maximum profit and efficiency, and the staffing strategy is a big part of that. I need to find a balance between having enough staff to provide excellent service and keeping labor costs manageable. After a lot of consideration, I've decided on a few key approaches.

Diary Entry: June 5th, 2021

The first decision was about the service model. I've chosen to go with a partial self-serve setup. Customers will order at the counter and pick up their drinks and food themselves. This reduces the need for a large waitstaff and keeps the operation lean. It also speeds up service, which is crucial for maintaining a high turnover during peak hours. However, I'll still have a few staff members dedicated to customer service—

keeping the space clean, answering questions, and ensuring that everyone feels welcome.

I've also decided on the number of staff I'll need to start with:

- **Baristas:** 3 baristas during peak hours (morning and early afternoon) to handle the rush, with 1-2 during quieter times.
- **Kitchen Staff:** 1-2 kitchen staff to prepare food items. I'm keeping the menu simple, so this should be manageable.
- **Front-of-House:** 1 staff member dedicated to customer service and maintaining the dining area. This person will also help with orders during peak times if needed.
- **Manager:** I've decided that I'll manage the cafe myself at the start, but as the business grows, I plan to hire a manager who can take over daily operations. This will allow me to focus on expanding the business or even starting new projects.

The next step is to start recruiting. I'm looking for people who are not just skilled but also passionate about sustainability and community. I want my team to feel as invested in the success of this cafe as I am. I'm planning to post job listings online and reach out to local networks. I'm hoping to attract students and young professionals who are looking for a part-time job that aligns with their values.

Diary Entry: June 10th, 2021

As I think more about the daily operations, I realize that the hours and days of operation are just as crucial to profitability as the staff. I need to maximize the cafe's revenue by being open when customers need us most, but without overextending myself or the team.

After analyzing the foot traffic in Mount Pleasant and considering my target market, I've decided on the following schedule:

- **Days of Operation:** Open 7 days a week. The cafe will operate every day because this maximizes the opportunity to serve customers, especially on weekends when foot traffic is highest.
- **Hours of Operation:**
    - **Weekdays (Monday to Friday):** 7:00 AM to 8:00 PM. These hours cater to early-morning commuters, students, and after-work crowds. The morning and lunch rushes are crucial, but staying open until 8:00 PM allows us to serve those who prefer a late coffee or early evening snack.
    - **Weekends (Saturday and Sunday):** 8:00 AM to 6:00 PM. Weekends typically have a more relaxed pace, with customers coming in for leisurely breakfasts or lunch. Closing earlier on weekends also gives staff some downtime and reduces labor costs during slower evening hours.

This schedule allows me to capture the most profitable times of the day while controlling overhead costs during quieter hours. It also provides consistency for customers, which is important for building a loyal customer base.

Diary Entry: June 15th, 2021

With the team starting to take shape and the operational hours decided, my attention has turned to the menu. I need to design it in a way that maximizes profits while still offering high-quality, sustainable products.

Here's what I've settled on:

- **Coffee and Beverages:**
    - **Specialty Coffees:** A range of espresso-based drinks, including lattes, cappuccinos, and flat whites. Prices will range from $4 to $6, with an emphasis on quality and sustainability. Offering a few unique seasonal drinks at a slightly higher price point ($6-$7) will help attract customers looking for something special.
    - **Tea and Cold Brews:** Offering a variety of teas, both hot and iced, as well as cold brew coffee, which has been popular in recent years. These drinks have lower overhead costs and can be priced between $3 and $5.
    - **Alternative Milks:** Offering non-dairy options like oat, almond, and soy milk for an additional $0.50 to $1.00. This caters to dietary preferences and increases the average ticket price.
- **Food Items:**
    - **Pastries and Quick Bites:** Muffins, croissants, cookies, and other baked goods sourced from local bakeries. These items

are low-cost and can be priced from $2 to $4, encouraging impulse buys.
- **Healthy Options:** Items like avocado toast, salads, and grain bowls, priced between $7 and $12. These appeal to health-conscious customers and justify a higher price point.
- **Warm Food:** Simple, warm options like soups and sandwiches, priced around $8 to $12. These can be prepared quickly, ensuring a fast turnaround during busy hours.

The goal is to have a mix of high-margin items (like coffee and baked goods) and more substantial offerings that can bring in higher revenue per customer. By keeping the menu relatively small, I can control inventory costs and reduce waste.

Diary Entry: June 20th, 2021

As we get closer to opening, I've also been considering the role of technology in optimizing operations. Investing in the right machines and systems can significantly impact both efficiency and profit margins.

Here's the plan:

- **Coffee Machines:** I'm investing in high-quality espresso machines that can handle the morning rush efficiently. While they're a significant upfront cost, they'll pay off by reducing preparation time and ensuring consistency.

- **POS System:** A modern, integrated POS system that handles both in-store and online orders. This will streamline operations, reduce errors, and provide valuable data on sales trends.
- **Partial Self-Serve:** By allowing customers to order and pick up their items at the counter, I can reduce labor costs and improve turnover. However, I'll still have staff available to assist and engage with customers, maintaining a personal touch.

This setup allows for a lean operation with minimal staff during off-peak hours while still providing excellent service during busy times.

Chapter 6 Summary and Next Steps:

In Chapter 6, Koo San carefully plans the staffing, operations, and menu of her cafe with a focus on maximizing profits and efficiency. She decides on a partial self-serve model to reduce labor costs, a mixed seating plan to balance turnover with customer comfort, and a carefully crafted menu designed to optimize revenue. She also sets operational hours that capture the most profitable times of the day and leverages technology to streamline processes.

The next chapter, "Sourcing Sustainable Ingredients," will focus on how Koo San finds local suppliers and ensures that her cafe's products align with her commitment to sustainability. She'll navigate the challenges of balancing quality with cost, building relationships with suppliers, and maintaining a menu that reflects her values.

Chapter 7: Sourcing Sustainable Ingredients

Diary Entry: June 25th, 2021

The cafe is really starting to come together, and now it's time to focus on what will truly set us apart—sourcing sustainable, high-quality ingredients. I've always been passionate about sustainability, and I want that commitment to be reflected in every aspect of the cafe, especially the food and drinks we serve.

Sourcing locally and sustainably isn't just a trend; it's a core value of my business. But I'm also aware that it can be more expensive, which means I need to be strategic about how I approach this. I've spent the last few days researching local farms, suppliers, and artisans who share my values and offer the kind of quality I'm looking for.

Diary Entry: June 30th, 2021

Today, I visited a local farmer's market to meet some of the suppliers I've been researching. It was an inspiring experience—seeing firsthand how much care and effort these farmers put into their products reaffirmed my decision to go local. I spoke with a few vendors who grow organic produce, and I'm considering them for the ingredients in our salads and grain bowls.

I'm particularly interested in working with a farm that's known for its heirloom vegetables and greens. Their produce is not only incredibly fresh but also unique, which could help differentiate my cafe's menu. We talked about the possibility of setting up a regular delivery schedule, which would ensure that I always have fresh, seasonal ingredients on hand.

Another exciting connection I made was with a local bakery that specializes in organic, whole-grain breads and pastries. Their products are exactly what I want to offer—delicious, wholesome, and made with care. We discussed a potential partnership where they would provide fresh baked goods daily, which would save me the cost and hassle of baking in-house while still offering top-quality items.

The challenge, of course, is balancing the higher cost of these sustainable ingredients with the need to keep menu prices competitive. I've been running the numbers, and while sourcing locally is more expensive, I believe that customers will be willing to pay a little more for food that's fresh, ethical, and supports local farmers. It's a matter of positioning the cafe as a place where quality and sustainability are worth the investment.

Diary Entry: July 5th, 2021

The more I delve into sourcing, the more I realize how crucial it is to build strong relationships with my suppliers. These relationships are the backbone of my business, ensuring that I get the best ingredients at a fair price and that my cafe has a reliable supply chain.

I've decided to focus on a few key partnerships:

- **Coffee Beans:** I've found a local roaster who sources beans directly from small, sustainable farms around the world. They're passionate about fair trade and quality, and their beans are roasted in small batches right here in Vancouver. It's more expensive than going with a big supplier, but the difference in taste and ethical sourcing is worth it. Plus, customers today are more discerning—they appreciate knowing where their coffee comes from.
- **Dairy and Alternative Milks:** I'm sourcing organic milk from a nearby dairy that's committed to humane farming practices. For non-dairy options, I've found a local company that makes small-batch oat and almond milk. These products are a bit pricier, but offering them aligns with the cafe's commitment to sustainability and gives us a competitive edge with health-conscious customers.
- **Fresh Produce:** The farm I connected with will supply the majority of our vegetables and greens. We've arranged for a seasonal rotation of

produce, which will keep the menu fresh and exciting. I'm also working with a local cooperative that aggregates products from various small farms, which ensures I have access to a wide range of fruits, herbs, and other ingredients.

By building these direct relationships, I can negotiate better prices and secure a consistent supply of high-quality ingredients. It also allows me to tell the story of where our food comes from, which I believe will resonate with our customers.

Diary Entry: July 10th, 2021

As I finalize the supplier agreements, I've also been thinking about the broader implications of sourcing sustainably. It's not just about the ingredients themselves—it's about reducing waste, supporting ethical practices, and creating a business model that's as environmentally friendly as possible.

One way I'm doing this is by minimizing food waste. I'm working with the kitchen staff to develop a menu that uses every part of the ingredients we buy. For example, vegetable scraps can be used to make stocks or garnishes, and any leftover bread from the bakery can be turned into croutons or bread pudding. It's a small step, but it makes a big difference in reducing waste and maximizing the value of every ingredient.

I'm also planning to implement a composting program. I've found a local composting service that picks up food scraps and organic waste, which will significantly reduce the cafe's landfill contributions. This not only aligns with our sustainability goals but also appeals to environmentally conscious customers.

Pricing the menu has been challenging, especially with the higher costs associated with these sustainable practices. However, I'm confident that customers will see the value in what we're offering. The key will be clear communication—letting people know exactly where their food and drinks are coming from, and why it's worth paying a little more for quality and sustainability.

Diary Entry: July 15th, 2021

With the suppliers and pricing strategy in place, the next step is to ensure that the staff understands and shares the cafe's commitment to sustainability. I've started planning training sessions where we'll go over the importance of sourcing locally, reducing waste, and educating customers about our practices.

I'm also considering ways to incorporate sustainability into the customer experience. For example, offering a discount to customers who bring their own reusable cups or containers is a simple way to encourage eco-friendly habits. Additionally, I'm planning to feature profiles of our suppliers on the cafe's website and social media, highlighting the people behind the products and the ethical practices they follow.

As we get closer to opening day, I'm feeling a mix of excitement and anxiety. There's still so much to do, but every day brings us closer to realizing this dream. Sourcing sustainable ingredients has been one of the most rewarding parts of the process, and I'm proud of the partnerships we've built. I'm confident that these choices will not only set us apart but also create a loyal customer base that values quality and sustainability as much as I do.

Chapter 7 Summary and Next Steps:

In Chapter 7, Koo San successfully sources sustainable ingredients by building strong relationships with local suppliers who share her commitment to quality and ethics. She carefully balances the higher costs of these ingredients with pricing strategies that reflect the cafe's values. The chapter also explores waste reduction, composting, and the importance of staff training in maintaining these sustainable practices.

The next chapter, "Marketing and Promotion," will focus on how Koo San creates a brand identity and develops a marketing strategy to attract customers to her cafe. She'll utilize social media, local events, and community engagement to build excitement for the grand opening and ensure a successful launch.

Chapter 8: Marketing and Promotion

Diary Entry: July 20th, 2021

With the cafe's opening just around the corner, it's time to shift my focus to marketing and promotion. I've put so much thought into the design, menu, and operations, and now I need to make sure people know about us. I've been researching marketing strategies that align with the cafe's values and will attract our target audience—students, young professionals, and the local community who care about sustainability and quality.

Diary Entry: July 25th, 2021

The first step in my marketing plan is creating a strong brand identity. I want the cafe's name, logo, and overall aesthetic to convey our commitment to sustainability, community, and quality. I've been working with a local graphic designer to develop a logo that reflects these values. We've settled on a clean, modern design with earthy tones that evoke the natural elements we're committed to preserving.

Next, I'm focusing on our online presence. I've started building a website that will showcase our menu, share the stories of our local suppliers, and highlight our sustainability practices. The website will also feature a blog where I can post updates, share recipes, and engage with customers. I'm also setting up social media accounts to connect with the local community. Instagram will be key for sharing photos of our dishes, the cafe's interior, and behind-the-scenes content that tells the story of our journey.

Diary Entry: July 30th, 2021

To build anticipation for the grand opening, I'm planning a series of promotions and events. I want to create buzz and get people talking about the cafe before we even open our doors.

Here's what I'm planning:

- **Soft Opening:** I'll host a soft opening a week before the official launch, inviting local influencers, bloggers, and community leaders to experience the cafe first. This will not only help spread the word but also give us a chance to test our operations and make any necessary adjustments.
- **Social Media Campaigns:** Leading up to the opening, I'll run a series of social media campaigns, including giveaways and contests. For example, I'll ask followers to share our posts or tag friends for a chance to win a free coffee or a meal on opening day. This will help build our online following and create excitement.
- **Community Engagement:** I'm reaching out to local organizations and schools to offer discounts or collaborations. For example, I'm considering a student discount to attract college students who are looking for a place to study or hang out. I'm also thinking about hosting workshops or talks on sustainability, which would align with our values and draw in customers interested in those topics.

Diary Entry: August 5th, 2021

As part of our marketing strategy, I'm also focusing on customer experience. It's not just about getting people through the door—it's about making sure they have a positive experience that keeps them coming back. I've been working with the staff to ensure that everyone is trained in customer service, including how to upsell menu items, offer recommendations, and create a welcoming atmosphere.

I've also implemented a loyalty program that rewards repeat customers. For every ten visits, customers can earn a free drink or a discount on a menu item. This encourages repeat business and builds a sense of community around the cafe.

Pricing is another important aspect of our marketing strategy. I've carefully considered our portion sizes and pricing to ensure that we're offering value while still maintaining profitability. The dishes are priced to reflect the quality of ingredients and the effort that goes into each one, but I'm also mindful of keeping them accessible. By offering a range of prices—from affordable breakfast items to slightly higher-priced lunch options—I can cater to different customer needs while optimizing revenue.

Chapter 9: Overcoming Setbacks

Diary Entry: August 10th, 2021

Despite all the planning, we've hit a few unexpected roadblocks. The final round of inspections revealed a minor issue with the ventilation system, which needs to be fixed before we can open. It's frustrating, especially since we were so close to the finish line, but I'm doing my best to stay calm and focused.

I've called in the contractors to address the issue immediately, and we're working overtime to get it resolved as quickly as possible. This delay might push back our opening date, but I'd rather have everything perfect than rush and compromise on quality or safety.

Diary Entry: August 15th, 2021

The ventilation issue has been resolved, but the delay has put additional pressure on the team. We're all feeling the strain of the last-minute changes, but I'm trying to keep morale high. I've reminded everyone that setbacks are a normal part of starting a business and that we've come too far to let this discourage us.

To keep the team motivated, I've decided to organize a small team-building event—a lunch outing at a nearby restaurant. It's a chance to step away from the stress for a few hours, bond as a team, and recharge before the final push.

One thing I've learned from this experience is the importance of flexibility and adaptability. No matter how well you plan, there will always be challenges. The key is to stay focused on the bigger picture and find solutions that keep you moving forward.

Diary Entry: August 20th, 2021

With the setback behind us, we're back on track for the opening. The extra time has actually given me a chance to refine the menu and streamline operations even further. I've standardized portion sizes and recipes to ensure consistency and reduce waste. I've also made a few adjustments to the pricing based on the latest cost analysis, ensuring that we maintain healthy profit margins while still offering value to customers.

I've also revisited the food prep strategy to make sure we're as efficient as possible. We've organized the kitchen layout to minimize movement and maximize productivity. Everything is labeled and stored in a way that makes it easy for the chefs to find what they need quickly. I've also refined the night-before prep process, so that when the chefs arrive in the morning, they can hit the ground running.

Chapter 10: Grand Opening

Diary Entry: August 25th, 2021

The grand opening is finally here, and I'm feeling a mix of excitement and nerves. We've worked so hard to get to this point, and now it's time to see if all our efforts will pay off. The soft opening went smoothly, with positive feedback from everyone who attended. I've made a few last-minute tweaks based on their suggestions, and I'm confident that we're ready.

The day started early, with the chefs and I arriving before dawn to make sure everything was prepped and ready. We've got a full staff on hand to handle the expected rush, and I've even called in an extra barista to help with the morning coffee orders. The team is pumped, and the cafe looks amazing—the living wall is thriving, the furniture is in place, and the menu is finalized.

Diary Entry: August 26th, 2021

Opening day was a huge success! We had a steady stream of customers all day, and the feedback was overwhelmingly positive. People loved the menu, especially the avocado toast and the quinoa bowls, which sold out by lunchtime. The coffee was a hit too, with many customers commenting on the quality and flavor of the beans.

The staff performed incredibly well under pressure, and the kitchen ran smoothly, thanks to the prep work and standardized recipes. We managed to keep wait times down, even during the busiest periods, and the partial self-serve model worked perfectly. Customers appreciated the quick service, and the mix of seating options kept the space feeling lively but not overcrowded.

Diary Entry: August 30th, 2021

As the first week comes to a close, I'm reflecting on everything we've accomplished. The cafe is off to a strong start, and the community response has been better than I could have hoped for. We've had a lot of repeat customers already, and the loyalty program is proving to be popular.

Looking ahead, I'm focusing on maintaining this momentum. I'll be keeping a close eye on sales data, customer feedback, and inventory levels to make sure we're running as efficiently as possible. I'm also planning to introduce a few seasonal specials next month, which will keep the menu fresh and encourage repeat visits.

I'm incredibly proud of what we've built—a cafe that not only serves delicious, sustainable food but also brings people together. It's been a challenging journey, but every setback and every late night has been worth it. This is just the beginning, and I'm excited to see where this journey takes us next.

Chapter Summaries and Conclusion

Chapter 8: Marketing and Promotion

- Koo San develops a strong brand identity, creates an online presence, and implements a series of promotional strategies to build anticipation for the grand opening. She focuses on community engagement, social media, and customer experience to attract and retain customers.

Chapter 9: Overcoming Setbacks

- Despite hitting unexpected roadblocks, including a delay caused by a ventilation issue, Koo San and her team adapt and overcome these challenges. She emphasizes the importance of flexibility, team morale, and efficient operations to stay on track.

Chapter 10: Grand Opening

- The grand opening is a success, with positive feedback from customers and smooth operations throughout the day. The cafe's strategic planning, menu design, and customer service pay off, leading to a strong start and a promising future.

Coffee Tasting Journal

Date: _____

Coffee Details

Coffee Name	Roaster	Origin	Roast Level	Brew Method
			(Light, Medium, Dark)	(Drip, Espresso, French Press, etc.)

Tasting Notes

Aroma	Intensity		Descriptors	
	(Mild, Moderate, Strong)		(Floral, Fruity, Nutty, Spicy, etc.)	
Flavor	Initial Taste	Mid-Palate	Finish	Descriptors
				(Citrus, Chocolate, Berry, etc.)
Body	Mouthfeel		Descriptors	
	(Thin, Smooth, Creamy, Full)		(Silky, Oily, Watery, etc.)	
Acidity	Level		Descriptors	
	(Low, Medium, High)		(Bright, Tangy, Sharp, etc.)	
Sweetness	Level		Descriptors	
	(Low, Medium, High)		(Sugary, Honeyed, Caramel, etc.)	
Aftertaste	Duration		Descriptors	
	(Short, Medium, Long)		(Pleasant, Bitter, Lingering, etc.)	

Overall Impressions

Balance	Complexity	Personal Rating
(Well-balanced, Overpowering, Muted)	(Simple, Moderate, Complex)	(Out of 10)
Additional Notes		

Notes:

Notes:

Notes:

Notes:

Notes:

Notes:

Notes:

Notes: